YOGA

Calm Minds

Written by
E.C. Andrews

Enslow
PUBLISHING

Published in 2025 by Enslow Publishing, LLC
2544 Clinton Street
Buffalo, NY 14224

Written by:
E.C. Andrews

Edited by:
Rebecca Phillips-Bartlett

Designed by:
Amelia Harris

Cataloging-in-Publication Data

Names: Andrews, E.C.
Title: Yoga / E.C. Andrews.
Description: Buffalo, NY : Enslow Publishing, 2025. | Series: Calm minds | Includes glossary and index.
Identifiers: ISBN 9781978541160 (pbk.) | ISBN 9781978541177 (library bound) | ISBN 9781978541184 (ebook)
Subjects: LCSH: Hatha yoga--Juvenile literature. | Mind and body--Juvenile literature.
Classification: LCC RA781.7 A537 2025 | DDC 613.7'046--dc23

Manufactured in the United States of America

CPSIA compliance information: Batch #CSENS25:
For further information contact Enslow Publishing LLC at 1-800-398-2504.

Please visit our website, www.enslowpublishing.com.
For a free color catalog of all our high-quality books, call toll free 1-800-398-2504 or fax 1-877-980-4454.

Find us on

Image Credits

All images are courtesy of Shutterstock.com, unless otherwise specified. With thanks to Getty Images, Thinkstock Photo and iStockphoto. Recurring images – Evgeniy Lebedeff, Mironov Konstantin. Cover – nu kristle, PeopleImages.com - Yuri A. 2–3 – wavebreakmedia. 4–5 – IONs, Pixel-Shot. 6–7 – wavebreakmedia, Adamov_d. 8–9 – fizkes, GOLFX. 10–11 – KlingSup , Natali Kuzina. 12–13 – Belavusava Alena, fizkes. 14–15 – narikan, maxicam, wowomnom. 16–17 – Gatot Adri, Rob Marmion, VectorShow. 18–19 – BearFotos, VGstockstudio, Illustratiostock. 20–21 – soumen82hazra, BalanceFormCreative. 22–23 – wavebreakmedia.

CONTENTS

Page 4	A Calm Mind
Page 6	Relax Your Brain
Page 8	Strengthen Your Body
Page 10	Remember to Breathe
Page 12	Warming Up
Page 14	Cat-Cow Pose
Page 16	Downward Dog Pose
Page 18	Bow Pose
Page 20	Child's Pose
Page 22	Healthy Mind and Body
Page 24	Glossary and Index

Words that look like this can be found in the glossary on page 24.

A CALM MIND

We all have feelings. There may be times when your emotions feel too big to control. There are ways to help make your big feelings seem less scary. One of them is yoga.

Yoga involves taking slow, deep breaths while stretching your body in different ways. Doing yoga can help you feel more relaxed and less anxious. Ten minutes of yoga before bed can help you sleep better.

Yoga comes from a religion called Hinduism, which started in India.

RELAX YOUR BRAIN

Yoga is a type of exercise, but it is not the kind that makes you feel out of breath. Yoga is slow and gentle. It should help you feel calmer and more focused.

Yoga involves holding your body in different positions. These positions are called poses. Concentrating on holding yoga poses while taking deep breaths can help focus your mind. This can make your thoughts seem clearer.

STRENGTHEN YOUR BODY

Yoga can help the rest of your body as well as your brain. Your body uses many different muscles when you stretch it and hold it in different poses.

Using your muscles often will help to keep them healthy. You may find that doing yoga makes you feel stronger. This will help give you more energy to get through the day.

REMEMBER TO BREATHE

Breathing is one of the most important things in yoga. Taking slow, deep breaths can help calm you down. This is part of what makes yoga so relaxing.

Before starting yoga, try some breathing exercises. Try breathing in through your nose for four seconds. Then breathe out from your mouth for five seconds. You should feel your tummy moving up and down as you breathe.

You should keep this up while doing your yoga poses.

WARMING UP

You will be stretching a lot while doing yoga, but it is still good to do some simpler stretches before you start. This will help you warm up and get your body ready for yoga.

Try stretching out your arms and reaching towards your toes. It is important that you only stretch as far as you are comfortable with. You can do this sitting down or standing up.

Try this after yoga too. You may find you can reach further!

CAT-COW POSE

A good pose to start with is the cat-cow pose. Start on your hands and knees. Lift your chin upwards. Push your shoulders and tailbone upwards and let your tummy relax towards the floor.

Breathe in through your nose as you do this.

Next, you can become a cat! You do this by tucking your chin towards your chest and arching your back towards the sky. Slowly breathe out through your mouth while you do this.

Where in your body are you feeling the stretches?

DOWNWARD DOG POSE

The downward dog pose stretches your arms and legs. Start on your hands and knees. Keeping your palms, fingers, and toes flat on the floor, slowly lift your knees off the ground.

Lift your knees until your feet are against the floor. Lift your heels a little if this is uncomfortable. Let your head and neck relax. Your body should look like an upside-down V.

BOW POSE

The bow pose stretches the front of your body. To get into the bow pose, start by lying on your tummy. Lift your chest and stretch your arms behind you towards your toes.

Grab hold of your ankles and hold the pose for 15 seconds. Breathe out as you let go of your ankles. Lie flat on your tummy and take a 20-second rest. Remember to keep breathing!

This pose makes your body look like a bow and arrow.

CHILD'S POSE

After doing a bow pose, it is important to rest your spine. Child's pose is perfect for this. To get into child's pose, kneel back on your heels with your big toes touching.

Keep your knees slightly apart. Lean forward to carefully rest your forehead on the floor in front of you. Rest your hands in a comfortable position at your side. Breathe and relax.

You can hold this pose for as long as you need to.

HEALTHY MIND AND BODY

While doing yoga, it is important to listen to your body. Only do what is comfortable for you. If you rush or stretch too much, you could get hurt. There is no hurry. Take your time.

Yoga is supposed to make you feel calm, relaxed, and focused. Yoga can help you feel more in control of your big feelings. Take your time and remember to breathe.

Has yoga helped bring your mind to a calmer place?

GLOSSARY

anxious	feeling nervous or worried
concentrating	giving complete attention to something that is happening
emotions	how people feel inside
energy	strength to be able to do things
focused	the feeling of giving complete attention to one task or goal
muscles	bundles of tissue that can contract or squeeze together
spine	the bones that run down the middle of the back and support the rest of the body
tailbone	the bottom of the spine

INDEX

bodies 5, 7–8, 12, 15, 17–19, 22
breaths 5–7, 10–11, 14–15, 19, 21, 23
exercises 6, 11
feelings 4–5, 23
hands 14, 16, 21
knees 14, 16–17, 21
poses 7–8, 11, 14, 16, 18–21
stretches 5, 8, 12–13, 15–18, 22